W9-CHE-768

LA LECHE LEAGUE INTERNATIONAL

Motherwise
101 Tips for a New Mother

BY ALICE BOLSTER

LA LECHE LEAGUE INTERNATIONAL
SCHAUMBURG, ILLINOIS USA

June 1997
©1997 La Leche League International
All Rights Reserved
Printed in the U.S.A.
ISBN 0-912500-23-9
Library of Congress 97-073188

Cover photo by David C. Arendt
Book and cover design, Digital Concepts, L.L.C.

La Leche League International
1400 N. Meacham Road
Schaumburg, Il 60173-4840 USA

To my husband, Bob, who is always there with wisdom, support, fun, and practical advice and to my boys, Max and Rhodes, who have shown me how to be a mother and given me more joy than I could ever have imagined.

Mother Knows Best

Dear New Mother,

    There is no one like you in your baby's life. You can see it in his eyes when he looks at you. You can see it when he contentedly falls asleep in your arms. You are the one who can comfort him when he is unhappy. You are the most important person in his life. No one will ever love him as you love him and no one will ever know him as you know him.

v

No one knows better than you what is best for your baby, but during the early weeks, you may not be sure. All new mothers have doubts and questions. That is why I have written this book. It is full of the kind of encouragement and support that I found to be helpful in raising my two children. The best advice I received encouraged me to do what was already in my heart. Take the suggestions that work for you. *You* know what is best for *your* baby. Trust yourself. You have the answers within yourself. You know best.

Tip #1

Good mothering is sometimes hard and
sometimes wonderful, but always worth it.

Tip #2

Find other mothers who speak to your heart and cultivate their friendship. Create a network of support with these mothers.

Tip #3

Don't let people persuade you to go against
your own heart. If advice feels wrong,
it probably is bad advice. Don't take it.

Tip #4

Enjoy all the moments with your baby.
They will go by faster than you think.

Tip #5

You know your baby better than anyone.
Don't be afraid to act on this knowledge.
Trust yourself.

Tip #6

For the first few weeks, don't expect to get anything done. If you get your teeth brushed and you take a shower, it's a good day.

Tip #7

Watch the baby instead of the clock.
Your baby will have his own rhythm as he
learns to live in our world. It's easiest if
you stay flexible and adapt yourself to
his schedule.

Tip #8

You have the answers within yourself.
Your instincts will guide you correctly.

Tip #9

People before things. Let your house be messy
while you take care of your baby.

Tip #10

Your alert, active participation in childbirth is
a help in getting off to a good start.

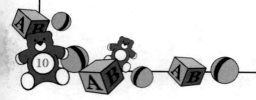

Tip #11

If your baby is crying, he is *not* trying to manipulate you; he has a need to be filled. Is he hungry? Even if he just nursed, put him to the breast anyway. Is he wet? Is he too cold or too hot? Does he need a change of position? Does he need a change of temperature or a

(More)

11

change of scenery? Does he need to burp? Is it time for a bowel movement? Does he need walking, rocking, or quiet? When you get to the end of the list, start over with these comfort measures.

Tip #12

The family is important and children are valuable. You are doing a wonderful thing by being a good mother.

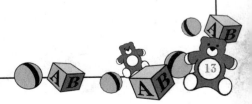

Tip #13

Remember that the advice you get from your friends or doctor may work for other babies but may not work for yours.

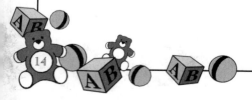

Tip #14

Don't be afraid to stand up for your baby's rights. He is depending on you to look out for him.

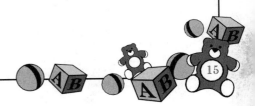

Tip #15

Of course babies are dependent. They need
you to feed them, they need you to cover
them when they are cold, they need you
to turn them when they are uncomfortable,

(More)

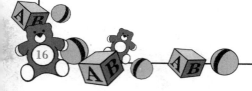

and they have only one signal to alert their mother that they need any of the above. Their mother is their key to survival; *of course* a baby is nervous when she is absent.

Tip #16

Take care of a need when it is appropriate and it won't surface later when it is not.

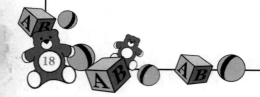

Tip #17

Your life will never be the same,
but that is not all bad.

19

Tip #18

Wear your bathrobe for the first week or so.
It will discourage well-meaning visitors from
staying too long.

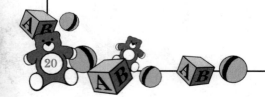

Tip #19

Was ever a sight so priceless as the first look
at your newborn child?

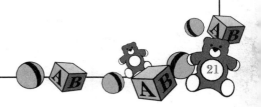

Tip #20

A baby's stomach is as big as a golf ball, the same size as his fist. Of course he seems to eat all the time. He's supposed to double his birth weight in five months. How much would you have to eat to do the same?

Tip #21

Feeding your baby is a time to relax, enjoy the moment, and take a break from the world.

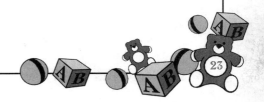

23

Tip #22

A new baby will recognize his mother right away by sight and smell and from then on will want no substitute.

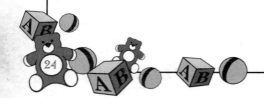

Tip #23

If you're late getting somewhere because of your baby, what better reason could you have?

25

Tip #24

Sometimes babies seem to cry a lot. Realize that your baby has a strong will to survive, and persistence in getting his needs met is a basic survival skill. Your job is to find out

(More)

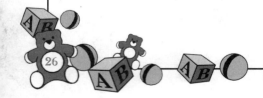

what your baby needs and to meet those needs. This approach may give you a new perspective on the situation so you don't get frustrated.

Tip #25

Mothering gets off to the best start when mothers have early and prolonged contact with their babies after birth. It is a good time to begin the introductions between mother and baby, even if you look like a wreck!

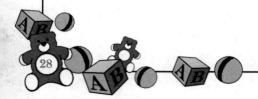

Tip #26

When you breastfeed, you aren't just "feeding" your baby, you are comforting and loving him, too.

Tip #27

Most babies do not sleep through the night.
Don't expect it! Enjoy the quiet moments
in the darkness when you and your baby are
the only ones awake.

Tip #28

Respond to your baby intuitively and without restraint. You will be a mother who is in tune with her baby. This rapport will make things easier through toddlerhood and childhood.

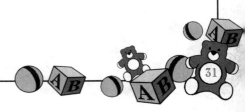

31

Tip #29

A baby's wants and needs are the same.
Learn to be sensitive to your own baby's
individual needs. He's not trying to
manipulate you, he *needs* you.

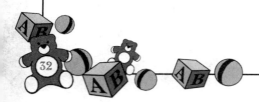

Tip #30

Mothering is not something you can learn
from a book—even this one!

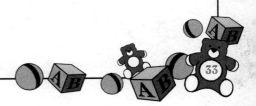

Tip #31

If you get help with your child or children,
look at the way the potential caregiver
responds to your child. A nurturing attitude
is the best qualification.

Tip #32

You never know what kind of baby you're
going to get. Stay open to the baby's cues.
If your schedule and the baby's schedule
don't mesh, it's easier for you to adjust
yours than for you to try to change
your baby's nature.

35

Tip #33

Never let the baby "cry it out." If you let him cry, he is learning several things. Distress is not followed by comfort, Mama cannot be depended upon or trusted, and his survival is not assured because his caregivers aren't around when he needs them.

Tip #34

A lot of your needs get put on hold when
you have a baby. You are more mature and
can deal with deprivation and disappointment
better than your baby. Don't expect him to
happily wait for you to get off the phone
to tend to him.

37

Tip #35

If you get help the first week, let the helper take care of the house while you take care of the baby.

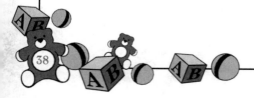

Tip #36

If people want to help, *let them.* Ask them to cook or come over and do a load of laundry, straighten up the living room, or go to the grocery store for you. If lots of friends want

(More)

39

to bring food, ask one of them to be the coordinator. Everyone can call her—instead of you—and she can schedule days for people to bring food, so that you don't get seven lasagnas.

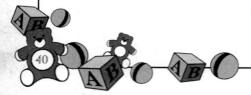

Tip #37

When you are breastfeeding, and want to practice nursing discreetly, nurse in front of a mirror or in front of a friend and ask if he or she can see any skin. Wear loose clothing that allows easy access for the baby.

Tip #38

Nursing your baby soon and often after birth
encourages milk production.

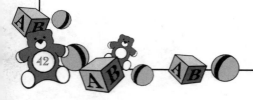

Tip #39

Respond to your baby without fear of spoiling him. A baby's needs and wants are the same. This is not the time to show the baby "who's the boss."

Tip #40

Get your hair cut a week or so before your
due date; you won't get another chance for
a while.

Tip #41

Sleep while the baby sleeps. Resist the
nagging thought that you should be getting
something done. Resting is what you need
to be doing.

Tip #42

Sleep with your baby. It makes no sense for you to get up out of a warm bed, walk across a cold floor, gather up a baby who is hysterical by that time, and sit in a rocking chair while you are nursing your baby. By that time, you are completely awake, tired, and resentful

(More)

46

about your sleep loss as you watch the clock. Keep a flashlight, diapers, and water for you to drink at the head of the bed. Unless the baby is crabby and needs to be walked, you're there until the next morning. You'll feel more rested and be a better mother for it.

Tip #43

Some babies like pacifiers, some don't.
Pacifiers are fine as long as you aren't giving
the baby a pacifier instead of your attention
and care. If your baby is breastfeeding, it is
best not to give any artificial nipples—

(More)

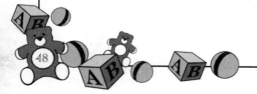

including pacifiers—for the first 3-4 weeks. The sucking action is different and can confuse the baby. When a baby that young is sucking, he needs to be getting nourishment.

Tip #44

I was happy to be my baby's pacifier while breastfeeding. I wanted him to know that people made him feel better, not things.

Tip #45

Keep your fingernails short. It is easy to scratch the baby. You can cut the baby's fingernails while he is asleep.

Tip #46

Simplify your life before your baby is born.
Resign from everything you can.
Don't be afraid to say,
"Once the baby comes, I'm out of here."

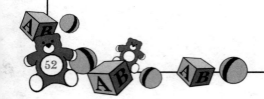

Tip #47

Have a phone installed near your bed and turn off the ringer. You can usually hear it ringing in another part of the house and can answer it if necessary or ignore it if you are busy with the baby or just falling asleep.

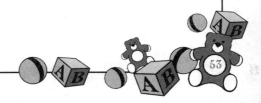

53

Tip #48

Purchase a soft cloth sling and try to get the baby used to it in the first month or so. Most babies love it and it will give you free hands for a little while. Be careful in the kitchen, though, around the stove and hot water.

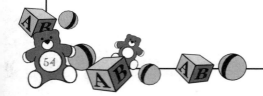

Tip #49

When the baby has a stable neck, toward the end of the first year, you can move to a backpack. It puts the baby at eye level with grown-ups, what fun! I found an extra one at a yard sale and kept one in the house and one in the car so I wouldn't have to remember it.

Tip #50

You will never regret the time you spend with
your children. It goes by more quickly than
you can ever imagine.

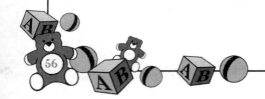

Tip #51

When you are at your wit's end over something, remember, "This too shall pass."

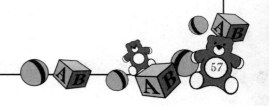

57

Tip #52

Nurture your relationship with your partner.
The stronger this relationship is, the more
secure your baby will be.

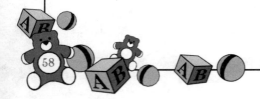

Tip #53

Try to be at peace with your partner, baby, and life in general when you go to bed. You'll sleep better if problems have been resolved.

Tip #54

Find good ways to relax at the end of the day.
Nurse your baby, spend a few quiet minutes
with your partner, talk with a friend on the
phone, or take a warm bath while the baby
sleeps or your partner holds him.

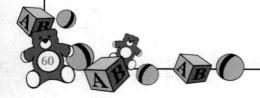

60

Tip #55

Get a tape of slow dancing music, hold the
baby while your partner holds you, and dance
with the lights turned down low.

61

Tip #56

Develop friendships with women who encourage your mothering instincts and avoid women who encourage you to suppress your instincts. You know those people, the ones

(More)

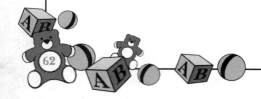

who tell you to let the baby cry it out, take a cruise and leave the baby with someone else, don't hold that baby so much, don't rock that baby to sleep—those people!

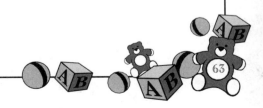

Tip #57

Raising good citizens is a worthy endeavor.
Society needs them, the world needs them,
and your children will need happy,
well-adjusted people to marry!

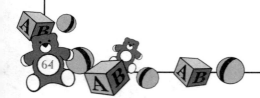

Tip #58

As mothers, we should try not to give our children our neuroses. Let them get their own—we worked hard for ours!

Tip #59

Your pediatrician received no more parenting training than you did. He learned how to take care of sick people, not how to raise happy, secure children. That's not to say that he won't have something valuable to offer; just evaluate it as you would any other piece of advice.

66

Tip #60

Talk to your baby. Even though he may not understand your words, he loves the sound of your voice.

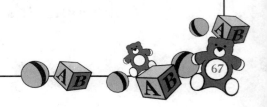

Tip #61

Wear your baby in a sling or carrier while grocery shopping. The chances are good that he will be happy and you will get your shopping done. If the baby gets fussy, find a quiet place to nurse him, then resume shopping. It's easier on everyone.

68

Tip #62

As your baby begins to coo and babble, respond to it. This provides his first speech lesson.

69

Tip #63

If the baby has a time of day when he is usually happy, try to do your errands then. Don't go when you are tired and hungry. If you are feeling good there is a better chance the baby will feel good and you'll have a nice outing.

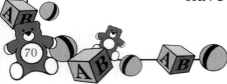

Tip #64

Taking care of yourself helps you to take better care of your baby. Don't skip meals. Keep lots of nutritious snacks on hand, eat plenty of fresh fruits and vegetables, and drink water or juice whenever you feel thirsty.

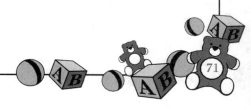

71

Tip #65

The tireder you get, or the angrier you get, try
to make your responses softer. It helps.

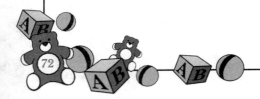

Tip #66

You are your baby's first love experience. Try to be to your baby what you want in your own love experience. You want someone who loves you unconditionally, whatever your mood. You want someone who is trustworthy,

(More)

73

predictable, stable, kind, and fun. You need to model for your baby the kind of love that will be healthy for him to have as an adult.

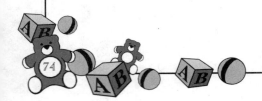

Tip #67

Even a less-than-perfect beginning can turn out fine. Don't get discouraged if things don't go as you had planned. Accept, adapt, regroup, love yourself, and go forward.

75

Tip #68

If you're going to take a trip and visit people you think may not be supportive of your mothering style, practice formulating responses to critical comments or questions. Spend time with a friend coming up with

(More)

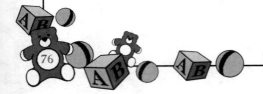

possible unsupportive remarks and deciding how you might respond to them. Being prepared might keep you from thinking afterward, "I wish I had said . . ." (or "I wish I *hadn't* said . . . !").

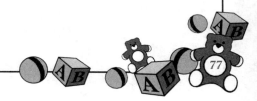

Tip #69

If people are really pushing you to do
something that feels wrong to you, you
can say "This is what works for me." Say this
over and over and they will finally give up.

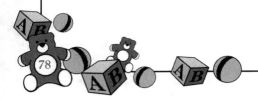

Tip #70

Practice enjoying the moment. We tend to live in the future, planning and thinking, "When the baby's asleep, I'll do . . . ," "After the baby is walking, I will . . . ," "When the baby is ten months, surely he'll be doing . . . ."

(More)

Train yourself to live in the present. This wonderful time will pass very quickly and will never come again. Relax and enjoy your baby.

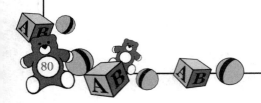

Tip #71

You are born with some mothering instinct, but it really develops as you and your baby grow together, love each other, and try to please each other.

Tip #72

The mother often sets the tone for the household. If you are crabby, chances are good that soon everyone in the house will be crabby, too. You don't have to stifle all your feelings when

(More)

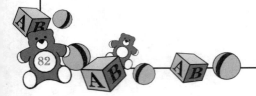

you are having a bad day, but you might consider the consequences of making your bad mood evident to your family. It doesn't sound fair, I know, but that's the way it is.

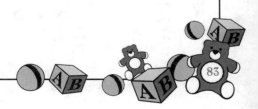

Tip #73

Do your best to "put on a happy face."
You want your children to feel that their
mother is basically a happy person. They tend
to see all grown-ups as serious and worry-
filled people. That's a pretty grim
way to see adulthood.

Tip #74

You can read all the child-rearing and parenting books you want, but watching and responding to your child is the best training. Your baby didn't read any of those books and none of the authors of those books ever met your baby.

Tip #75

When your friends call to help, try to spread
it out over the first few months. You'll still
welcome an extra pair of hands when your
baby is two months old.

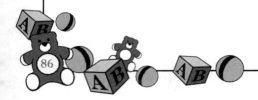

Tip #76

Mothering is easier the second time around. You have gotten rid of all your preconceived ideas, so you can relax and respond to your baby's uniqueness.

Tip #77

Human infants are the most dependent of all
creatures and for the longest amount of time.
We would not have survived as a species if
cave mothers had put their offspring in
another part of the cave at night or left them

(More)

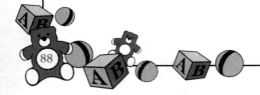

for long periods of time during the day.
We may have the means to separate ourselves
from our young, but biologically, we weren't
meant to and it still upsets the baby and
the mother.

Tip #78

Your partner is not going to handle the baby exactly the same as you. On the one hand, this may drive you crazy. On the other hand, the baby will have a different relationship with his father than the baby has with you.

(More)

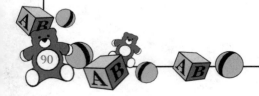

The baby will learn to use different signals with his father than he uses with you. As long as the baby is lovingly cared for and not allowed to cry, this difference is okay. This may be hard for the mother to learn.

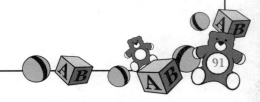

91

Tip #79

When it comes to housework,
lower your standards!

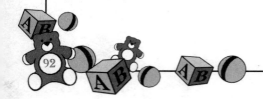

Tip #80

The first baby in a family is really brave to come first and show his mother how to do it!

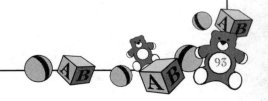

Tip #81

Don't apologize for the state of your house, clothes, yard, or kitchen. You are taking care of your baby which is the most important job that you could have. If you are criticized, just agree with the person. It's probably true any

(More)

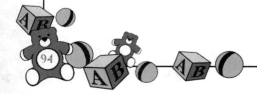

way. Just say "You're right! The living room is a mess!" It takes all the fun out of trying to make you feel guilty and maybe they'll leave you alone.

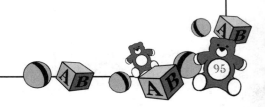

95

Tip #82

Until you have a baby, you have no idea how
much you can love someone.

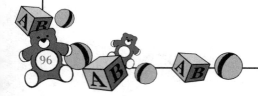

Tip #83

What a baby learns first is not love, but trust.
He learns that he can trust his mother and
father to give him what he needs. If you
establish this trust in infancy, it will still be
there when your baby is a teenager.

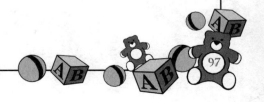

Tip #84

The hardest thing to teach a child is to come
to you when he is in trouble.

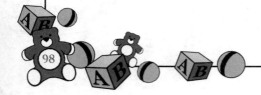

Tip #85

You don't "lose your identity" by being "just a mother." You gain a whole new one.

Tip #86

You're not just raising a child, you are raising your grandchildren's mother or father. If you set a good example now, you'll have less to correct later.

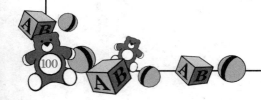

Tip #87

Try to remember what it was like to be small and helpless. Respond to your baby as you were nurtured or as you wish you had been nurtured.

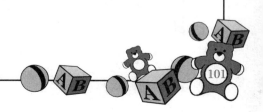

Tip #88

Being a mother is a chance to pass on the good things your parents gave to you. It's also a chance to avoid any bad parenting habits that you may have observed in your parents.

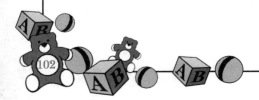

Tip #89

Problems and frustrations arise when you try to lead your life after your babies are born as you did before they were born.

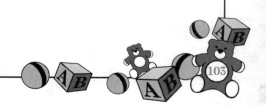

Tip #90

Do the best you can, then let it go. While we all strive for the ideal in cleaning our home, in meals we present our family, and in our relationships, the ideal is rarely attainable. Don't beat yourself up about it.

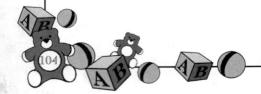

104

Tip #91

Babies and children need intensive and individual nurturing. If they get this they will flourish and become happy people with good self-esteem who are good company and a joy to parent.

105

Tip #92

If you've had all you can take, give your baby
to your partner and take a walk, a bath, or do
something else that helps you relax. If you
are by yourself, put the baby in a sling and
go for a walk. Fresh air can dispel a
lot of irritation.

Tip #93

Run a quick check on yourself if you start to
feel crabby. Am I tired? Am I hungry? Am I
expecting something unrealistic from my
baby? Do I feel cooped up and need a walk?
Am I coming down with a cold?
Identifying the source of irritability is the
fastest way to get rid of it.

107

Tip #94

If your baby or toddler wakes up crying, he
may not be ready to wake up yet. Nurse or
rock him back to sleep to finish his rest.

Tip #95

If your baby has a particular time of the day when he is sometimes fussy, try to leave that time open to care for him. For example, get dinner ready in the morning and put it in the refrigerator, or get snacks ready for children

(More)

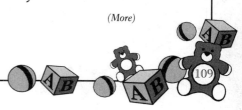

109

who will be coming home from school. Do whatever you can think of that will make life easier for you during this time when your baby is often unsettled.

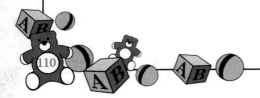

Tip #96

If you take your baby to a party or some other gathering, you don't have to let *everyone* hold your baby. Do not be intimidated. It is strictly your decision. When someone asks to hold your baby, you can always say, "I think he's

(More)

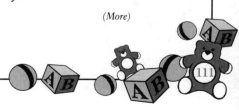

111

visited enough. I'll just keep him, thanks anyway" or "I'm not ready to give him up yet." Your loyalty is to your baby, not to great-aunt Nancy or your genuinely sweet and well-meaning friends.

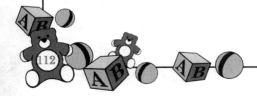

Tip #97

A telephone answering machine is an ideal
baby gift. Use it when you are busy with the
baby and don't want to answer the phone.

Tip #98

Don't neglect your spiritual side. Take a
moment every day to center yourself.

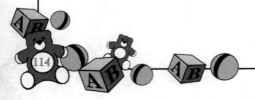

Tip #99

We need to teach by example the lessons we want our children to learn. It is important for a child to experience fairness, consideration, patience, and joy if he is to have these attributes as an adult.

115

Tip #100

If a baby is ready to do something—
like wean, sleep through the night, walk, talk,
potty train—you can't stop him. If he isn't
ready, you can't make him. Well, you can,
but you pay for it later.

Tip #101

"No matter how far our world advances technologically, the decisions of how to use that technology still have to be made by people. And so the kind of people we produce is crucial to the direction our world takes.

(More)

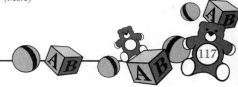

117

You know that raising a loving, caring child is the most important contribution any of us can make to the progress of the world."

— Marian Tompson,
co-Founder of La Leche League International

For Further Reading

Many of the following books are sold through the La Leche League International Catalogue. To order additional copies of *Motherwise* or to request a free catalogue, call 1-800-LALECHE or call the Order Department at 847-519-9585.

The Womanly Art of Breastfeeding
by La Leche League International
(6th edition, 1997)
This definitive guide provides breastfeeding information for mothers with a warm, supportive, practical approach.

Breastfeeding Pure and Simple
by Gwen Gotsch
(La Leche League International, 1994)
Provides new mothers with a basic introduction that will guide them through the early months of their nursing relationship.

By Martha and William Sears:
25 Things Every New Mother Should Know
(Harvard Common Press, 1995)
While providing information on everything from giving birth to breastfeeding to meeting baby's needs, this book reinforces a mother's confidence by assuring her that she is the expert on her baby.

The Baby Book: Everything You Need to Know About Your Baby from Birth to Age Two (Little, Brown, 1993)
Emphasizes baby's basic needs and helps new parents to meet those needs through a loving, nurturing, attachment style of parenting.

By Dr. William Sears:

Growing Together: A Parent's Guide to Baby's First Year
(La Leche League International, 1987)
Charts the development of a tiny newborn into a curious toddler and teaches parents to enhance their baby's development through their responsiveness.

Becoming A Father: How to Nurture and Enjoy Your Family
(La Leche League International, 1986)
Addressing the joys and problems of parenthood from a father's perspective, Dr. Sears writes from experience about the ways in which a child can help strengthen a marriage and bring about increased love and maturity.

Nighttime Parenting: How to Get Your Baby and Child to Sleep
(La Leche League International, 1985)
Explains the differences in babies' sleeping patterns compared to those of adults and introduces a style of nighttime parenting to help put an end to sleep problems.

The Fussy Baby: How To Bring Out the Best in Your High-Need Child
(NAL Dutton, 1989)
Discusses ways to nurture babies who are "high need" and require extra attention from parents.

How To Really Love Your Child
by Ross Campbell (Victor Books, 1992)
Focuses on the importance of showing children that they are loved through eye contact, physical contact, and focused attention.

Infant Massage: A Handbook for Loving Parents by Vimala Schneider McClure (Bantam, 1989)
An illustrated guide to a warm and special way to interact with your baby—the gentle art of massage.

A Good Birth, A Safe Birth: Choosing and Having the Childbirth Experience You Want by Diane Korte and Roberta Scaer (Harvard Common Press, 1992)
Discusses the pros and cons of today's childbirth options, teaches expectant parents how to make sure their wishes are followed, and discusses the use of medications and painkillers.

Being There: The Benefits of a Stay-at-Home Parent by Isabelle Fox (Barron's, 1996)
Reveals startling evidence about the critical importance of a parent's presence in a child's early years and discusses ways to provide the necessary consistency when a substitute caregiver must be used.

The Family Bed: An Age-Old Concept in Child Rearing by Tine Thevenin
Explores the pros and cons of sharing a family bed and suggests that sleeping together will help solve bedtime problems and create closer family bonds.

About La Leche League International

For forty years, La Leche League International has been committed to helping mothers worldwide to breastfeed through mother-to-mother support, encouragement, information, and education, and to promoting a better understanding of breastfeeding as an important element in the healthy development of the baby and mother. LLL Groups meet monthly in communities around the world, giving women a place to share breastfeeding and mothering experiences and to gather the knowledge and support they need to continue breastfeeding.

Call 1-800-LALECHE to request a free catalogue, to receive breastfeeding support, or to find out about LLL Groups near you, or write to La Leche League International, 1400 North Meacham Road, Schaumburg IL 60173 USA. Visit La Leche League's web site at www.lalecheleague.org/